D0734547

KNOW
CAN DO!

KNOW CAN DO!

Put Your Know-How into Action

Ken Blanchard

Paul J. Meyer

Dick Ruhe

BERRETT–KOEHLER PUBLISHERS, INC.
San Francisco

Berrett-Koehler Publishers, Inc.
235 Montgomery Street, Suite 650
San Francisco, CA 94104-2916
Tel: (415) 288-0260   Fax: (415) 362-2512   www.bkconnection.com

Ordering Information
Quantity sales. Special discounts are available on quantity purchases by corporations,
associations, and others. For details, contact the "Special Sales Department" at the
Berrett-Koehler address above.
Individual sales. Berrett-Koehler publications are available through most bookstores.
They can also be ordered directly from Berrett-Koehler:
Tel: (800) 929-2929; Fax: (802) 864-7626; www.bkconnection.com
Orders for college textbook/course adoption use. Please contact Berrett-Koehler:
Tel: (800) 929-2929; Fax: (802) 864-7626.
Orders by U.S. trade bookstores and wholesalers. Please contact Ingram Publisher
Services, Tel: (800) 509-4887; Fax: (800) 838-1149;
E-mail: customer.service@ingrampublisherservices.com; or visit
www.ingrampublisherservices.com/ordering for details about electronic ordering.

Production Management: Michael Bass Associates

Berrett-Koehler and the BK logo are registered trademarks of Berrett-Koehler
Publishers, Inc.

Printed in the United States of America

Berrett-Koehler books are printed on long-lasting acid-free paper. When it is available,
we choose paper that has been manufactured by environmentally responsible processes.
These may include using trees grown in sustainable forests, incorporating recycled paper,
minimizing chlorine in bleaching, or recycling the energy produced at the paper mill.

Library of Congress Cataloging-in-Publication Data

Blanchard, Kenneth H.
    Know can do!: put your know-how into action / Ken Blanchard,
Paul J. Meyer, Dick Ruhe.
        p. cm.
    ISBN 978-1-57675-468-9 (hardcover: alk. paper)
    1. Organizational learning. 2. Active learning. 3. Performance.
4. Employee empowerment. 5. Organizational effectiveness. I. Meyer, Paul J. II.
Ruhe, Dick. III. Title. IV. Title: Know-how into action.
HD58.82.B57 2007
658.3'124—dc22

                                                                    2007021624

First Edition
12 11 10 09 08 07   10 9 8 7 6 5 4 3 2

CONTENTS

PREFACE

When I think about the writing of *Know Can Do*, it's been a long time coming and has quite a history. Years ago, a dear friend of mine asked me what my biggest disappointment was with my career. That thoughtful question motivated some real self-reflection.

That's when I realized that what bothered me the most was that my work did not have universal, lasting impact. While my books were widely read, many people did not follow through on the concepts and use them consistently in their day-to-day work. My concern was that some managers seemed to be content merely to talk about leadership practices, rather than actually implementing them.

My friend said, "Maybe you're looking in the wrong place. You're trying to change people's behavior only from the outside." He went on to say that he used to do the same until he realized that lasting change in people's behavior starts on the inside and moves out.

I knew right away he was right, because all I had been focusing on were leadership methods and behavior. I hadn't focused much on what was in people's heads or hearts.

Armed with this new insight, I realized that I needed some way to close the knowing-doing gap—a way that focused on the inside as well as the outside.

Enter Paul J. Meyer.

Paul has been a trailblazer in the behavior change business for almost fifty years. His Success Motivation Institute, Inc., founded in 1960, is dedicated to "motivating people to their full potential." When I explained my dilemma to Paul, he was excited about trying to solve it. Give Paul Meyer a challenge, and you have a focused person beyond your belief.

After thinking about it, Paul prepared a keynote speech for a big international company on whose board he serves. The speech was entitled "The Missing Link"—what is needed to put the know-how you gain from reading books, listening to audios, watching videos, or attending seminars into action. That was the beginning of *Know Can Do*.

Working with Paul on this project was a real joy. He is an entrepreneur extraordinaire who has founded more than forty companies with worldwide sales that exceed $2 billion. With more than forty books in print, in some circles I am considered an author extraordinaire. What we needed to complete our team was a spokesperson who was willing to travel near and far to spread the word.

The person who came immediately to my mind was Dick Ruhe. He has worked with our company for almost twenty years and has been our number one speaker, carrying our message around the world. Dick had done some writing of his own, but as a speaker extraordinaire, he was the perfect match to work with Paul and me on *Know Can Do*.

One plus one plus one has turned into far beyond three. We are excited about *Know Can Do* and hope it gives you and your organization the strategies you need to take the knowledge you are taught and put it into action. We know it only takes one diet to lose weight—the one you focus on. In the same way, we think *Know Can Do* can make a real difference by giving people simple tools to close the knowing-doing gap and make their knowledge come alive. May our dreams come true and your goals be accomplished.

—Ken Blanchard
June 2007

THE PROBLEM

There once was a successful author who wrote about simple truths. His books were designed to help himself and others manage and motivate people in more effective ways.

Everyone who read his books loved his stories and messages. He sold millions of copies. Yet there was one thing that troubled him.

It usually reared its head when someone told him, "I've read all your books and really love them."

The author had always been taught that true learning involves a change in your behavior. In fact, he thought that learning was a journey from knowing to doing. So if the person praising his work commented about a particular favorite concept, he usually asked, "How has knowing that changed the way you behave?"

Most people had a hard time answering that question. As a result, they often changed the subject by talking about another concept or some other book they were reading.

These kinds of interactions led the author to conclude that the gap between what people know—information they have picked up from books, audios, videos, and seminars—and what they do—how much they apply and use that knowledge—was significant. He found that was particularly true today with the incredible technology that makes knowledge easily accessible to everyone. People, he concluded, tend to spend considerably more time acquiring new information than developing strategies to use their newly acquired knowledge in their daily lives.

In his seminars the author tried everything he could think of to get people to be true learners and apply and use what he was attempting to teach them. To help them focus, he urged everyone to do three things he'd learned in graduate school from a professor who had been researching how to study for years.

The first thing the professor taught him was to insist that students take notes. Unless a person is one of the 0.0001 percent of the population who has photographic ears, listening alone will not make that person learn. In fact, three hours after a seminar or class, pure listeners will remember only about 50 percent of what they just heard. Twenty-four hours later, they will have forgotten 50 percent of that. At the end of one month, they will have less than 5 percent recall of the new material they were exposed to at the seminar.

The author confirmed this every time he was asked to speak at an annual company meeting. He always asked the audience, "Who talked to you last year?" They would scratch their heads.

"What did the speaker talk about?" he would then ask. People in the audience would strain to remember the subject, with no recall of what they actually had heard. So he always emphasized taking notes in his seminars.

The second thing the author did was to urge participants to reread their notes within twenty-four hours and summarize what he liked to call their "aha's" or key insights. He suggested that they either write them in clear, neat handwriting in a notebook or save them in their computers. Why did he insist they summarize their notes in clear, neat handwriting if they preferred a notebook to a computer? Because he found that after a seminar, the few people who did take notes would file them rather than review them. Later, when someone would say, "You went to that seminar—what was it all about?" they would open their file and—lo and behold—they couldn't even read their own handwriting. Their notes were useless.

Finally, he prodded participants to pass the knowledge on. He suggested that within a week of arriving home from the training, they schedule a conference room and invite everyone who was important in their world of work to come for half a day, so they could teach them the aha's they'd gleaned from the seminar. The author knew that one of the best ways to begin to apply new knowledge was to teach it.

Yet few, if any, participants really followed through on these suggestions. They just seemed to be too busy when they got back to work. This reinforced the problem: it is difficult to get people to use and apply knowledge they have recently gained.

Disappointed but not discouraged, the author continued to search for answers to close the knowing-doing gap. He visited universities and talked to professors. He visited corporations and talked to training directors. He visited foundations and talked to learning officers. They all identified with the problem, but none had a good answer. He started to wonder if he'd ever find the real answer.

Then one evening after dinner the author came across an article in a back issue of *Fortune* magazine about the legendary businessman Phil Murray, who owned and operated a number of profitable companies. He read about Murray's history as a successful entrepreneur, but that is not what attracted the author to him. What intrigued the author was Murray's long history as a guru in the personal development industry. What he found particularly interesting were the comments from people who had bought the entrepreneur's programs. The article cited case after case of people who claimed that what they were taught in Murray's programs had changed their lives.

"They actually used their new knowledge!" the author said aloud.

The next morning the author found the entrepreneur's Web site and called the contact number for his office, which luckily was headquartered only an hour away. An executive assistant named Evelyn told the author that Murray wasn't there; he and his wife were at their cabin in North Carolina. When Evelyn found out who the author was, she insisted that he call Mr. Murray at his cabin.

"I don't want to disturb his vacation with a work-related matter," said the author.

"Don't worry about it," said Evelyn with a laugh. "Phil's confused about the difference between work and play. He has reached the point in his life where he really enjoys helping others. I know he'd love to hear from you."

THE MISSING LINK

W hen the author called the entrepreneur's cabin, he was greeted with a warm, hearty hello.

After introducing himself, the author said, "I'm sorry to disturb you at your cabin, Mr. Murray, but your assistant Evelyn told me you wouldn't mind answering a few questions."

"Please, call me Phil," the entrepreneur said. "And by the way, I'm a big fan of your books."

Within a couple of minutes, the author felt like he was talking to an old friend. When the author explained why he was calling, he could sense Phil's excitement.

"I've been interested for a long time in 'the missing link,'" said the entrepreneur.

"The what?" the author asked.

"The missing link," repeated Phil. "That's what's lacking in the learning process when we just read books, listen to CDs, or attend seminars."

"The missing link—that's exactly what I want to find," said the author. "People seem to enjoy the books I write, the CDs and videos we produce, and the seminars I conduct, yet I don't see a lot of people actually using what they learn. The gap between what people know and what they do is driving me crazy!"

"Tell me about it!" The entrepreneur's hearty laugh came through the phone loud and clear. "Getting people to actually use information they have acquired requires change, and change does not come easily."

"Usually not," said the author.

"There are three reasons why people don't learn and start doing what they know. The first reason is this: **information overload**. They suffer from an overdose of knowledge. This is a common trap to fall into because it is easy to read a new book, listen to a new CD, or go to a new seminar. Knowledge comes easy, but that will not bring about change in behavior."

The author nodded. "I suppose you're right. I guess it's more fun to find out about something new than struggle to use what you now know. Maybe that's why we've become knowledge junkies."

"It's more fun to acquire knowledge than apply it, but that's not the only reason people don't do what they know. The second reason might surprise you, but here it is: **negative filtering**. People have a dysfunctional processing system, or, to put it another way, they suffer from stinkin' thinkin'. Whenever they learn something positive, even about themselves, they put it down or discount it. This negative attitude continually holds them back, and, as you no doubt have witnessed, attitudes are tough to change. Without a positive, open attitude, particularly toward learning, you're never going to close the knowing-doing gap."

"So what I hear you saying," said the author, "is that we commonly substitute increased knowledge for change, because knowledge is so easy to get. Then our negative thinking comes into play and undermines our motivation to use what we now know."

"You're a quick study," said the entrepreneur. "The third and final reason why we don't use what we know is **lack of follow-up**. For example, how many smokers don't already know that smoking is bad for them?"

"I don't think any, probably," the author said.

"Don't most of the smokers you know have a positive attitude toward giving it up?" asked Phil.

"Come to think of it, they do."

"Then why don't people stop smoking? Because it's hard. The habit is ingrained into the fabric of their lives. Changing habits or behavior requires a real concentrated effort. Yet most people don't know how to follow up their good intentions to break the habit and change their behavior."

"As I listen to you," said the author, "I get the feeling that closing the knowing-doing gap is not only difficult but complicated."

"Honestly, it's not that complicated," said Phil. Once you really understand the three reasons people don't do what they know, everything will become clear. Then you'll be able to help people bring about wanted change in their own lives by using exponentially more of the knowledge available from books, audios, videos, and seminars. The key to doing that is **repetition, repetition, repetition**! It's the missing link."

"So *repetition* is the missing link between what people know and what they actually do?" asked the author.

"It sure is," said Phil. "Repetition is the key to overcoming each of the reasons people don't do what they know."

In the background, the author could hear a child's voice calling, "Grandpa."

"I'd certainly be interested in hearing more about that," said the author, "but I've already kept you too long. It sounds like you're in demand."

"Tell you what," said the entrepreneur with warmth in his voice, "why don't you come visit me in a couple of weeks? I'll be back home then, and we can go into more depth about the importance of repetition and how it can improve our acquisition of knowledge, our attitudes, and our behavior."

"You've got a deal," said the author. "Your executive assistant Evelyn and I are already buddies, so I'll make arrangements with her."

"I look forward to it," said the entrepreneur.

THE POWER OF REPETITION

Two weeks later, the author was sitting in the living room of Phil Murray's home. The whole place was elegantly casual, far more modest than a man of his means could afford. A wall of windows, however, offered an inspiring view of a deep, green valley ringed by rugged foothills.

"You said the key to overcoming the three reasons that people don't do what they know is repetition," said the author. "Could you tell me more about that?"

"I said repetition, repetition, repetition!" insisted the entrepreneur. "When I emphasize repetition like that, what I'm really referring to is what we call *spaced repetition.*"

"Spaced repetition?" wondered the author aloud.

"That's right," said Phil. "Spaced repetition is a learning technique where you don't learn something in just one sitting. You're exposed to the information periodically over time, so that it sinks in."

"Tell me more," said the author.

"Some people call spaced repetition *behavioral conditioning* or *internal reinforcement*. My good friend John Haggai calls it 'the mother of all skills' and 'the mother of permanent change.' That's because one statement makes little if any permanent impact on someone. It has to be repeated over and over again. Not immediately, but after a period of time for reflection.

"Advertisers use this technique all the time," Phil continued. "They call these repetitions 'impressions.' They've found that it takes a number of exposures before people identify with what they are selling and become willing to take action."

The author thought about this as he gazed at a hawk flying high above the valley. "So a person who understands the power of repetition has a decided advantage, then," he said.

"No doubt about it," Murray replied. "It is difficult to change a belief, send a voter to the ballot box, or influence a person to contribute to charity through one interaction. We do not make people see, feel, or do something in one sentence. An important message almost always requires repetition over time if it's going to have its intended result."

REASON 1:
Information Overload

"**Y**ou mentioned that the first reason we don't do what we know is that we suffer from information overload," said the author. "We simply have too much knowledge. How does spaced repetition affect that?"

"Good question," Phil said. "Information overload leads to some real problems. It immobilizes us."

"That's painful to hear," said the author. "I just experienced that very thing recently at a golf school. I'm a golf nut, so I decided to go to a three-day school to improve my game. But I got the opposite result—I got worse."

"Really?"

"Yes. They taught me too much. When I got back home and tried to play, I was awful. I had paralysis by analysis. I was working on so many things at the same time I became immobilized."

"I've heard about that," said the entrepreneur. "It must have been discouraging."

"Given what you know about information overload, what good is it to read one book after another or attend seminar after seminar?" asked the author.

"There's nothing wrong with reading books and attending seminars," Murray replied. "These are fundamental learning tools, and we need them. The problem comes when we expose ourselves to new knowledge all the time with no pause for integrating our new know-how and putting it into action. If we continue to expose ourselves this way, we become brain cluttered. This is why so many people are drowning in a sea of information."

"So what's the answer?" asked the author.

"Let me answer your question with a question," said Phil. "Why doesn't a fish drown when it is constantly swimming in a drowning environment?"

"Interesting question," said the author with a smile. "Could fish be smarter than we are?"

"Not really," said the entrepreneur with a laugh. "But they do have a built-in monitoring system that helps them take from the water only what they need and nothing else. Something we as human beings could use when it comes to dealing with the overwhelming amount of information available to us today."

"It sounds like a matter of focus," said the author.

"I think you're right," the entrepreneur replied. "We have to decide what we need to learn to help us perform better and then go about it with vigor."

"It's interesting," said the author. "A friend of mine, Denny, went to a golf school recently that was very different from the one I attended, and he's playing much better."

"That must frost you," said Phil. "What was the difference in the two schools?"

"Exactly what we are talking about," said the author. "The difference was focus. The first day they analyzed all parts of his game on video. Then they picked three or four learning goals for him while he was at the school, and they would not teach him one more new thing until he graduated."

"Graduated?" asked Phil.

"To graduate from a learning goal, he had to hit ten shots. On each shot, he had to tell one of their pros whether he was doing what they had taught him or not. If he wasn't, he had to tell them how he needed to correct his error for the next shot."

"Good example," said the entrepreneur. "They made sure he could use what they had taught him. Daniel Webster, the originator of Webster's dictionary, said that he preferred to totally master a few good books rather than read widely. To drive the point home, to totally master something, I think it's imperative that we bathe in it until we saturate our entire being. We must slowly chew and digest it until it becomes a part of us."

"I think that's a little over the top, but I get the point," said the author. "You're emphatic about that. It sounds like our friend, spaced repetition."

"It sure is," said the entrepreneur. "It's been said that your mental constitution is more affected by a small amount of material thoroughly mastered through spaced repetition than by twenty books you read only once. The habit of attending a seminar only one time or reading a book once, while exposing yourself to new information, just builds the habit of forgetting. We are training ourselves to know and not do. It's really the exact opposite of what we should be doing."

"Could you tell me more about the habit of forgetting? I do have a tendency to forget a lot of what I read and hear."

"The human mind—everyone's, including yours and mine—is in the constant process of doing one of two things: it's either learning something new or forgetting. If we neglect something, we soon forget it. When we focus on something with spaced repetition, we remember it."

"Does that mean there's no value in attending a good seminar just once?"

"Of course there is some value," said Phil, "but attending the same seminar a number of times with a pen and notepad would be better than just once. It's one way you can escape the 'forgettery process.' The same has also been said about a book. Read it again and again, underlining it, highlighting it, and writing down key ideas. Then review your learnings again."

"So it sounds like you don't do the same thing when you read a book or go to a seminar a second or third time."

"Absolutely," said Phil. "The first time I read a book I decide I want to learn from, I just read it straight through to get a sense of it. The second time I read it and underline the key concepts. The third time I might take notes. The fourth time I could choose to read it with a learning partner. And it is important to do all this over a period of time. We all have to develop our own strategy to keep our interest and zero in on what we want to apply and use in our lives."

"Is all that really necessary?" asked the author.

"Unfortunately, yes, from my experience," said Phil. "To truly master an area, people should immerse themselves in a focused amount of information, rather than be exposed to a large amount."

"And they should do it repeatedly, is what I hear you saying," said the author.

"Yes," said the entrepreneur. "People should learn less information more often, rather than learn more information less often."

"Do you mean, for example, that rather than reading a large number of books, people should read a smaller number of books more times?" asked the author.

"Yes," said the entrepreneur, "spaced repetition is the key, and

People Should

Learn

Less More

And Not

More Less

"How has knowing this impacted the way you train people in your companies?" asked the author.

"Why don't you go to our office and talk to Dwayne Harper, our director of training and development, and find out? Turn right coming out of our driveway and go about five miles. The corporate headquarters for our company is on the left. Evelyn will make an appointment with Dwayne for you."

Phil Murray sent the author off with a firm handshake. "Come on back after you've met Dwayne, and we can have lunch together."

"Will do," said the author.

APPLYING THE LESS-MORE
PHILOSOPHY

When the author arrived at Dwayne's office, he found an elder statesman who had been working with the entrepreneur for many years. Dwayne had an easy style and grace that was inviting. When he smiled and told the author to have a seat in the discussion area of his office, the author felt privileged.

"So Phil's been talking to you about closing the learning-doing gap," Dwayne said.

"He sure has," said the author. "I've seen how people—including myself—have a real challenge closing that gap. Phil says that people have to learn less more."

Dwayne smiled. "That philosophy drives everything we do in our training, development, and educational efforts in all the companies that the entrepreneur owns."

"What do you think about that philosophy?" asked the author. "Does it really work?"

Dwayne nodded. "Before I started working with Phil, I was the typical training director. I spent more time looking for the next new management concept than I did following up what I'd just taught our people. I would help design a tremendous training program, run everybody through it, and then look for the next new training idea. The way I judged my effectiveness was by attitudinal evaluations that participants filled out at the end of a seminar about how they liked it. We always got high grades, but the trainings weren't all that effective. People didn't really apply what we were teaching them."

"How did you change that?" asked the author.

"When we learned from Phil that less learned more is best, we began to concentrate on a few key concepts we felt people should learn. Spaced repetition became our motto. Now we teach important concepts over and over again, until they become ingrained in the way people think and behave."

"So you're spending more time following up training than creating new training programs?"

"Yes," said Dwayne. "We spend significantly more time on follow-up than we do designing, organizing, and delivering our training. And we think our people are better trained than anyone, anywhere."

It sounded good, but the author was skeptical. "Could you give me an example?" he asked.

"Sure," said Dwayne. "A number of years ago, we decided that we wanted to create legendary customer service. We didn't want to merely satisfy customers—we wanted to blow them away. When you deliver legendary service, customers are so excited about how you treat them that they want to brag about you. They become part of your sales force. We decided this would be an ongoing effort. We would drill deep, teaching less more, and repeat the teaching again and again."

The author raised an eyebrow. "So how's that working for you?" he asked.

"We've seen measurable—and sometimes dramatic—results in both customer and employee satisfaction. We're constantly training and updating our people on new ideas about how to give legendary customer service. If any new concept comes along in customer service, we integrate it into what we are already doing, rather than sending our people off in a different direction."

"That's interesting," said the author. "I gave a speech at a company recently, and they had a big banner behind me on the stage that said, 'The Year of the Customer.' When I saw it, I laughed and said, 'What's next year?' After talking to you, I'm sure you know why I said that. It seemed to me that every year should be the year of your customer. After talking to you and Phil, I guess the way you make that happen is to reinforce the message year after year through spaced repetition."

"Absolutely," said Dwayne. "That's why we're constantly pushing our people to get better at delivering legendary service. We give our people the best customer service books we can find each year and have everyone read them several times, continuing to cull useful information from them. We want to apply what we read if it makes sense to us.

"Everyone also goes through a two-day legendary service training program every year. The concepts we teach are the same, but we teach them differently each year. We also bring in some new concepts but make sure they are well integrated into what they learned last year. As training director, I keep reinforcing the message until our people's knowledge turns into a positive attitude, and that good attitude turns into behavior that creates raving fan customers who sing our praises."

"Sounds like a good strategy," said the author.

"It's a strategy that can lead to quantum leaps for our company," Dwayne said. "We want our people to know what they are doing so well that they can almost go on automatic pilot. When that occurs, they can make something big happen."

"What do you mean?" asked the author.

"If people thoroughly know what we are trying to accomplish with our customers and they've completely mastered every aspect of their jobs, they don't have to think about their responsibilities. Their minds are free to watch for opportunities to create stories that will blow our customers away."

"Can you give me an example?"

"Sure," said Dwayne. "One great example comes from the front desk of our corporate headquarters, where people are greeted and the phones are answered. Our front desk people call themselves 'Directors of First Impressions.' They are constantly thinking of ways they can get to know our customers, anticipate their needs, and become their friends, both when they walk in our corporate headquarters and when they call us on the phone. For example, we tell them that when the light goes on to indicate there's a call, they should calm themselves, recognizing that they have a service opportunity. Particularly when someone calls to complain."

27

"When you say 'service opportunity,' what do you mean?" asked the author.

"That will be clear when you hear my story," said Dwayne. "Last week I saw Stephanie, one of our Directors of First Impressions. She had a big smile on her face as I approached. I asked her what was going on, and she told me she had a great story to share. The day before, she'd been answering phones. She said when the phone rang and the light went on, she'd quieted herself down, remembering that this was a service opportunity. No sooner did she pick up the phone than this guy started yelling into her ear.

"'I'm your worst nightmare!' the guy shouted at her. Without losing a beat she said, 'Is that you, Alex?' When he said, 'Who's Alex?' she shouted back, 'My ex-husband!'"

Dwayne chuckled at the memory. "Stephanie said it totally diffused the guy's anger. He howled with laughter. Turns out the guy had an ex-wife who was a nightmare, too. She and the customer became good buddies after that."

"Sounds like Stephanie has a pretty quick wit," the author remarked.

"Yes," said Dwayne. "I asked her how she came up with that so quickly. She said that ever since she'd gotten the idea that every call was an opportunity to serve, she'd been getting more and more creative. So when the man started yelling at her, the first person she thought of was her ex-husband."

The author nodded. "I'm beginning to get the power of what you're saying," he said. "Once people have really mastered their jobs through the less-more philosophy and spaced repetition, they can get creative and become extraordinary."

As the author's conversation wound down with Dwayne, he thanked him for his time. On the way back to Phil's home for lunch, he realized that he had already learned a great deal.

A short time later the author arrived at Phil's house. As he turned into the driveway, he made a mental note to carve out some time to go to the golf school his friend had attended. It fit into what he was learning from the entrepreneur, and it might not hurt his game, either. Before he got out of the car, he got out a little notebook and wrote in clear, neat handwriting some summary notes on what he had learned about information overload:

Reason Why People Don't Put Their Know-How into Action #1: *Information Overload*

♦ We retain only a small fraction of what we read and hear only once.

♦ Therefore, we should read and learn *less more* and not *more less*.

♦ To master something, we should focus on a few key concepts, repeat them over time, immerse ourselves deeply in them, and expand on the ideas and skills. Spaced repetition is key.

♦ Once people have mastered their jobs, they are better able to be creative and make big things happen.

REASON 2:
Negative Filtering

A fter Phil greeted the author, he led him to the family dining room, where a beautiful lunch of salmon and rice pilaf had been prepared.

As they sat down to eat, the entrepreneur said, "Are you getting the kind of information you wanted?"

"Yes," said the author, "but what I need to do is write the information down and review it over and over, don't I?"

"As I said before, you're a quicker learner!" said Phil.

The author said, "I think I understand how focus and repetition overcome the first reason why people don't do what they know. I'm ready to hear about the second reason. Didn't you say it had something to do with stinkin' thinkin'?"

The entrepreneur smiled. "You're right. People are often too negative, which gives them an inadequate filtering system. Let me ask you a question. Is positive thinking more powerful than negative thinking?"

"Yes, I would say so," said the author.

"Then tell me," said Phil, "is it a choice? Do you get to choose between positive thinking and negative thinking?"

"Of course you do," said the author.

"Then why don't most people choose positive thinking over negative thinking?"

The author took a drink of his water, pondering his answer. "That's a good question," he replied. "Now that you mention it, negative thinking is much more prevalent among people than positive thinking. I wonder why."

Phil was quiet for a moment. "We're often programmed that way," he said at last.

"How so?" asked the author.

"When we come into the world, we are completely dependent on our parents or surrogate parents—those who choose to raise us. And we have no choice about who these people are or what our circumstances will be. Right from the beginning, I think all of us are searching for unconditional love. We don't want to be loved conditionally, depending on what we do or say on any given day. We want to be loved for who we are. Unfortunately, all the people who are gathered around us—our parents and other adults—haven't necessarily gotten this kind of unconditional love themselves, which makes it hard for them to give it. Thus, they tend to love us conditionally, based on our behavior. So we are constantly trying to do things to gain approval and a sense of belonging."

"How does this relate to negative thinking?" asked the author.

"As kids, we tried to get attention through our achievements, seeking praise and approval from our parents. It was a frustrating process, because, like all of us, our parents tended to accentuate the negative rather than the positive. When we behaved well, they expected it and therefore didn't say anything. When we did something wrong, they jumped all over us."

"But don't you think it's important to correct kids when they're off course?" the author asked.

"Sure," said Phil, "but not without positive reinforcement, too. When we don't get caught doing anything right, we start to doubt ourselves and doubt others. We begin setting up defense mechanisms to protect ourselves. We start filtering everything that comes to us through a mind that is totally dominated by negative thinking. Our minds become closed. We adopt judgmental attitudes and our insights are fear driven."

"I had great parents," said the author. "I don't think they always caught me doing things wrong."

"So you feel really good about yourself."

"Generally," said the author, "but I still have my doubts and fears about myself."

"Where did you pick those up?" asked Phil.

"Probably in school. I didn't learn like all the other kids and often got bored with school. That got me in trouble. On top of that, I wasn't a very good reader and some of the teachers used to make me read in front of the class. It was embarrassing, particularly when I mispronounced some of the words."

"That's interesting," said Phil. "How did you get to be a writer?"

"That's a story in and of itself. I wasn't supposed to be good at that, either. But I got interested in leadership and then got some opportunities to teach. One thing led to another, and then I took a leadership course from my department chairman. I wanted to audit his course, but he insisted I take it for credit. This involved not only taking tests but also writing papers. He was right. I learned a lot.

"At the end of the semester, he asked me to write a textbook with him. He had been teaching leadership for ten years but was a nervous wreck about writing. Since he thought I was a good writer, he figured we'd be a great team. He was the first person to ever praise my writing. With that encouragement, I sat down with him, and over the next year we wrote a textbook that is still used today, almost forty years later."

"His encouragement was really important, wasn't it?" asked Phil.

"It sure was. When you've written a book, people think you can write, and then you get other opportunities. Pretty soon I realized that all that negative stuff they had told me about myself in school wasn't true. In time I became a best-selling author."

"It took you a while to overcome all that negative programming, didn't it, though?" asked Phil.

"I guess you're right about that. It's interesting. My parents accented the positive with me, but a number of people at school bombarded me with negative programming about my reading and writing skills."

Phil smiled. "As you can tell from your own example, if you had listened to and believed all the negative things people said, you wouldn't have achieved half of what you've accomplished. You should feel good about that." The entrepreneur reached for the bread basket and offered it to the author.

"Thanks," said the author, helping himself to a slice. "Two things are becoming clear as we talk. First of all, one person who shows confidence in you can make all the difference in the world. Second, we have a choice about who we're going to listen to. If I'd listened to all the naysayers in my life, I might have accepted a less challenging job and have limited expectations for myself. An encouraging word was all I needed to climb out of the negative box I'd been put in."

"You were lucky," said Phil. "A lot of people are so beaten down that they can't hear positive feed-back when it comes their way. They discount it.

"It's sad, but most people can't overcome the kind of negative conditioning you went through," said Phil with a sigh. "They achieve only a small percentage of what they could, because they accept too little too soon, and everything is filtered through their negative thinking and their closed, judgmental mind-set."

"I'm glad I was one of the lucky few. The right person came into my life at the right time. But when you put all the things you've been talking about together, it does look discouraging," said the author.

"It could be," agreed the entrepreneur. "Compared with what our Creator had in mind for us, we often live our lives under a cloud of negative thinking. We put on a judge's robe when we read, listen, and watch everything, which is totally unfair to our minds, our hearts and our futures. It's the worst case of self-abuse. It's hard to be a learner if your filtering system is damaged."

"So how exactly does a negative, closed mind-set affect learning?" asked the author.

The entrepreneur thought for a moment. "What happens is that only an extremely small percentage of the information we receive has a chance to be remembered, let alone be allowed into our sub-conscious mind, accepted, and then actually applied and put to use. When we read a book, listen to an audio, watch a video, or attend a seminar, we are reading and listening with our present mental attitude, which in many cases is focused on worry, indecision, negative thinking, prejudgment, opin-ionated thinking, et cetera. All the things that people say and the sound that occurs around us is 100 percent of what is available for us to hear. The books and other literature we choose to peruse is 100 percent of what is available to enter our minds through reading. But with a closed, negative mind-set, by the time information that we hear or read encounters the mental traffic in our subconscious—where we can accept, believe, understand, and use it—only about 10 percent gets through. It's like a ten-lane freeway converging into a single lane. What do you think is the result?"

"A traffic jam," said the author. "Is there any way to break up that traffic jam and improve that percentage?" asked the author. "To get the traffic flowing again, as it were?"

"Yes, there is," said the entrepreneur. "And it's a skill that can literally revolutionize your life."

LISTENING WITH A POSITIVE MINDSET

"The solution to retaining more of what you learn is to listen with an open, positive mindset," said the entrepreneur. "I'll give you some pointers on listening this way." He got up from the lunch table, found a pad of paper, and wrote:

LISTEN

◆ with no prejudice or preconceived ideas,

◆ with a learning attitude that is excited about new information,

◆ with positive expectancy,

◆ with a pen in hand taking notes,

- with a desire to hear not only what's being said, but also what it can trigger in your imagination,

- with a "How can I use this?" attitude.

"This type of mind-set can spark an 'aha!' experience that can give you the last number in the combination to the vault of life that you've been looking for," said Phil.

The author had been listening closely. "What you're suggesting," he said, "is that if I have a positive filtering system, instead of getting only 10 percent of what I'm hearing and reading, I will probably learn much more than I'd ever anticipated."

"You're getting it," said Phil with a smile. "That often means you see connections to other things you've been exposed to, including ways you can apply your knowledge that you never thought of before. But that requires being open to new information, wherever it may come from. That's the way we grow best—with an open, positive mind. Seeds planted on good soil produce many times what is sown.

"This is what excites me," continued the entrepreneur, "because it leads to possibility thinking. Instead of getting 100 percent of what you are reading or hearing, your open mind allows you to increase your knowledge many times more. Not only do you clear that traffic jam, you open up whole new roads. Sometimes you leave the road altogether and start flying, because an open, positive filtering system can ignite our creativity, ingenuity, and resourcefulness. We can create possibilities way beyond our wildest dreams."

"I wonder if that explains why we see people every once in a while who far outperform others," said the author, "not just doubling their performance, but outdoing their performance a hundred to one."

"Yes," said the entrepreneur. "These are possibility thinkers. People who are open to new information and who are constantly looking to apply that new information in ways far beyond what their teacher, mentor, or coach ever imagined. They are possibility listeners, possibility participants, and possibility doers. A possibility mind-set not only can lead to a permanent change of attitude but also can impact performance and results."

"Have you ever had a personal experience of the power of possibility thinking?" asked the author.

"I sure have," said Phil. "One Sunday I came out of church all fired up. I was in an incredibly creative mood. I turned on the radio in my car and heard a song that inspired me. I pulled off the road and made an outline of a lesson for one of the courses I planned to teach. That course eventually turned out to be the flagship of our product line and our best-selling program for more than thirty years, bringing in over $100 million in profits. The fact that I had a positive attitude was the main reason this happened. If I'd attended the service with a negative attitude and been negative about the preacher, sermon, or music, I would have gotten stuck in the mental traffic jam like everybody else. But I had the lanes wide open that day, which took me to places I'd never even dreamed of."

"Sounds like possibility thinking has really impacted your life and your business."

"It certainly has," said Phil.

To the author, it was all sounding too good to be true. "But even possibility thinking can only get you so far," he said. "Aren't some things just impossible?"

"Possibility thinkers do the 'impossible' with great regularity," replied the entrepreneur. "Possibility thinking was involved when Roger Bannister broke the four-minute mile on May 6, 1954. They said it wasn't humanly possible, but Bannister ran the mile in 3 minutes and 59.4 seconds. That was unbelievable in 1954. But once it happened, within seven weeks John Landy hit 3 minutes and 57.9

seconds. In the next fifteen years, Roger Bannister's record was beaten 260 times by men in 177 races. Jim Ryun, as a senior in high school in Kansas, beat Bannister's record in 1965 with a time of 3 minutes and 55.3 seconds. Once breaking the four-minute barrier was repeated over and over again, it was seen as doable and in that process it changed the nature of the thinking about the four-minute mile from negative—*it can't be done*—to positive—*I can do it*."

The author said, "You make a good case for having a positive mind-set, Phil. Not just because it will help people learn more but also because it creates possibility thinkers who can accomplish great things and even alter history."

"It's important to remember, though, that even with a positive, possibility mind-set, repetition is required. Only after a number of people beat Bannister's record did naysayers become yay-sayers. We've come to understand that 62 percent of all ideas are accepted only after they are—" To finish his sentence, Phil turned to a fresh page in his notebook and wrote:

presented

presented

presented

presented

presented

presented

The author nodded thoughtfully. "I think I know what you mean. The way I overcame the negative programming I got in school looked something like this." He pulled a pen from his pocket and wrote:

I can't write

I can't write

I can't write

I can write

I can write

I'm an author!

The entrepreneur said, "It's interesting that presenting things six times seems to be the secret to spaced repetition."

"Why do you think that's so?"

"I've found that when people are first exposed to a new idea, they reject it, because it conflicts with their preconceived ideas. The second time they're exposed to a new idea, they resist it, because they can't accept it. The third time they're exposed to a new idea they partially accept it but have reservations as to its use. The fourth time people are exposed to a new idea, they fully accept it, because they feel it expresses what they've been thinking. The fifth time they're exposed to a new idea, they partially assimilate it, by using it themselves. The sixth time they're exposed to a new idea, they fully assimilate it by owning it and passing it along to others."

The entrepreneur rose from the table. "I have some handouts on this from my seminars. Follow me."

Phil led the author into his home office and pulled some papers from his file cabinet.

"This is how it works," he said as he gave the hand-out to the author. It read:

From Rejection to Assimilation

First exposure: REJECTION.

"I reject it because it conflicts with my preconceived ideas."

Second exposure: RESISTANCE.

"Well, I understand it, but I can't accept it."

Third exposure: PARTIAL ACCEPTANCE.

"I agree with the idea, but have reservations as to its use."

Fourth exposure: FULL ACCEPTANCE.

"You know, that idea expresses the same way I've been thinking."

Fifth Exposure: PARTIAL ASSIMILATION.

"I used that idea today. It's terrific!"

Sixth Exposure: FULL ASSIMILATION.

"I gave that idea to one of my sales people yesterday. In the truest sense of the word, the idea now belongs to me."

"Thanks," said the author. "This will be very useful. But let me ask you something. After I broke through the negative filtering around my writing, I seemed to develop a much more positive attitude toward a lot of things. Do you always have to go through that six-step process?"

"No, there's a shortcut," said Phil. "The more positive experiences you have with positive thinking, you are able to go through the six steps almost automatically and creative ideas begin to spring up almost instantaneously. Eventually you move toward being an inverted paranoid like me."

"What's an inverted paranoid?" the author asked.

"Inverted paranoids are people who think the world has conspired to do only good for them. That's really the ultimate result of becoming a positive thinker. But it's a journey. And sometimes people need help along the way."

The author thought about that for a moment. "Can you give me an example of someone in your organization who previously had a dysfunctional filtering system and changed into a positive, possibility thinker?" he asked.

"Yes, I can, and I'll introduce you to her. She's Suzanne Alcott, our chief operating officer. Suzanne is one of the brightest young women I know and a great COO, but she was driving me and everybody on my management team crazy because she was the ultimate negative thinker. She tossed a wet blanket on every new idea."

The author smiled. "Aren't chief operating officers supposed to do that?" he asked. "Their job is to make sure you do things right."

"As protectors of the operation, sure, they need to know how to say no. But Suzanne was draining everyone's energy. Since then, her turnaround has been fabulous. Why don't you go and talk with her?"

"I'd love to meet her," said the author.

"You know where to get an appointment. And why don't I meet you in my office tomorrow, so we can process what you've learned?"

USING GREEN LIGHT
THINKING

W hen the author arrived at Suzanne Alcott's
office, he found a bright, energetic young
woman who was excited to share her story with him.

"Phil always sends people to me nowadays when
he wants to illustrate a change from a negative to
a positive mind-set," she said with a good-natured
laugh.

"I'm eager to learn about it," said the author.

"As I'm sure Phil told you, I was the wet blanket
on every new idea. I went way beyond the typical job
description of a skeptical chief operating officer.
Luckily, at the end of my first year, Phil had a pull-
no-punches performance review meeting with me."

"Pull no punches?" the author said quizzically.

"Yep," said Suzanne. "He was very caring but
frank and direct. He said, 'Suzanne, you're one of
the best chief operating officers I have ever known.

You know your field, and I can count on you to make sure we do things the right way. But your negative, critical mind-set is driving me and everyone on our team crazy. Therefore, the number one goal I want to set with you next year is changing that mind-set.'

"I told Phil I heard him loud and clear, but I didn't know how I would accomplish that goal.

"'From now on,' he told me, 'every time you and I meet or you're part of any team meeting, I want you to be in charge of Green Light Thinking.'

"I had no idea what he meant by Green Light Thinking," said Suzanne, "so I asked him what it was. He told me:

"'When any new idea or project proposal is presented in a meeting, your job will be to start the discussion about why you think that idea or project is something that we should do. In other words, you will be our lead 'go for it' person. You will hold off giving any negative response until every positive, creative thought has been received from the group. If you're meeting with me one-on-one, I want to hear your possibility thinking.'"

Suzanne shook her head and continued, "That was a mind-boggling assignment for me, but I knew I didn't have any choice. Phil wanted me to win, but he also wasn't willing for me to continue with what he called a negative filtering system."

"Were you ever able to raise any objections in meetings?" the author asked.

"Yes," said Suzanne. "During meetings that Phil and I had with our team, Yellow Light Thinking was permitted to follow Green Light Thinking. While I could not be the *first* one to make a cautionary comment, we were all encouraged to give our best feedback. But negative responses were never to precede positive responses."

"How did that process work for you?" asked the author.

"It was amazing," said Suzanne. "In the beginning, I could feel myself resisting. But after a while, that changed. Because I had to focus so much on positive possibilities, when it came to putting up any yellow or red flags, I had trouble thinking of any. My focus had changed that much."

"Are you still able to function well as a COO who some of the time has to say no?" the author asked.

Suzanne nodded. "I think so, and so does Phil. But I'm much more pleasant to be around now that I've become a real creative possibility thinker. Without the structure of the Green Light then Yellow Light Thinking, I doubt I could have pulled it off."

"Did you get any other benefits from this process?"

"Yes, I gained credibility," said Suzanne. "When I did express a concern during Yellow Light Thinking, people listened to me much more. Since I was no longer Miss No Can Do, they took my negative feedback more seriously."

● ● ●

On his way out of Suzanne's office the author stopped to see Evelyn to schedule his meeting with Phil the next day.

She smiled and said, "Sounds like he's putting you through the paces."

"That's for sure," said the author with a laugh.

As he walked to his car, his mind was going a mile a minute. *I need to relax*, he thought. Fortunately, he had scheduled a golf game with Denny, the friend who had attended the golf school that focused on only a few things to learn.

It was a beautiful day to play golf, and the first two holes went well for both the author and Denny. On the third hole, the author hit his second shot into a sand trap. As he approached the trap, the author said to his friend, "I hate sand traps. That's the worst part of my game."

"Why would you program your mind with that kind of negative thinking?' Denny asked. "At the golf school I attended, they told me if you think you aren't good at some part of your game, guess what? You won't be very good at it. Try something for me."

"All right, Mr. Know-It-All," the author said.

"When you enter the trap, say to yourself out loud, 'I love the sand. I'm one of the best sand trap players around.' And then walk into the trap acting like you are."

Although he felt foolish, the author did exactly what Denny told him. Surprisingly, when he got to the ball, he felt really comfortable standing over it. He swung the club, hitting the sand a couple of inches behind the ball, and watched as it floated out of the trap, hit a couple of feet in front of the cup, and rolled into the hole.

"Nothing to it!" he shouted to Denny. Then they both burst into laughter.

"I know this stuff works, but I didn't expect it to happen quite so quickly," said Denny as they walked onto the green to retrieve the author's ball.

"Neither did I," said the author, "but I spent all morning learning about the power of positive thinking."

That night as the author relaxed at home, he summarized what he had learned from Phil, Suzanne, and, he reluctantly admitted, his buddy Denny:

Reason Why People Don't Put Their Know-How into Action #2: *Negative Filtering*

◆ Because we don't get unconditional love and support when we are young, we begin to doubt ourselves and doubt others.

◆ Self-doubt causes us to filter all information—whether in book, audio, video, seminar, or conversation format—through our indecisive, closed-minded, judgmental, critical, fear-ridden mind-set, which leads to negative thinking.

◆ Negative thinking causes us to
  • learn and use only a small fraction of what we see and hear;
  • achieve only a small percentage of what we could achieve;
  • accept too little too soon.

◆ We grow best with a positive, open mind that ignites our creativity, ingenuity, and resourcefulness and creates possibilities beyond our expectations.

◆ We must find ways to become ready and willing to open our minds. Instead of trying to find what's *wrong* in the new information, we need to be Green Light Thinkers who actively seek out what's *right* and say to ourselves: "I know there is something of value in what I'm reading or hearing; what is it?"

◆ Changing a closed, negative mind-set to an open, positive mind-set cannot be left to chance. Once we commit to changing, we need a specific strategy that continually reinforces our new way of thinking.

⚬   ⚬   ⚬

The following morning the author arrived at Phil Murray's corporate office for their next meeting. When Phil came out to greet him, he was bright-eyed and ready to go. "Come on in," Phil said as he waved him inside.

Just like his house, Phil's corporate office was comfortable but far more modest than the typical office of a top executive. The walls were lined with tastefully framed sports memorabilia and well-stocked bookcases. A circular table sat next to a large window that overlooked a serene woodland setting.

The author couldn't wait to tell Phil about his golf experience and gave him an exciting recap as he settled into a chair at the table.

"Nice birdie," said Phil. "Sounds like getting rid of your stinkin' thinkin' immediately improved your performance. How did you enjoy your meeting with Suzanne?"

"Very enlightening," said the author. "I love Green Light Thinking."

"That strategy certainly gave Suzanne time to develop a new way to think and sort out information," the entrepreneur commented.

"Apparently so," said the author. "She even told me that now she has trouble providing good negative or cautionary feedback."

"Don't let her fool you," said Phil. "When push comes to shove, she can still put holes in any good argument. But she's also become one of the best supporters of new ideas and projects. She's a big promoter of our Office of the Future."

"Office of the Future? I have no idea what that is," admitted the author. "Could you explain?"

"Sure," said Phil. "About a decade ago I realized that things are changing so fast in the world today that we have to manage the present and create the future at the same time. I realized it wasn't a good idea to have the same people managing your present who are planning your future. If you do, people with present-time responsibilities will kill the future, because they're either overwhelmed with the present or have vested interests in it."

"That's interesting," said the author. "I imagine you don't find many people who are good at both future and present-time thinking."

"That's for sure," said Phil. "As a result, I designated my wife, Alice, as the head of the Office of the Future. She's one of the most positive possibility thinkers I know. She has on her staff three other people who have nothing to do with the day-to-day operation of any of our enterprises. Their entire job is to look into the future and attempt to see what will be happening with technology and other innovations that could disrupt any of our businesses. They really saved us in our training and development business after 9/11."

"A lot of businesses took a hit after 9/11," said the author. "Most people didn't want to travel then."

"They sure didn't," said the entrepreneur. "But Alice and her staff had been looking at teleconferencing, e-learning, virtual meetings, and all kinds of exciting opportunities. In fact, recently two of our trainers were in our conference building from one to three in the morning, training 120 managers across Europe in six different countries on the telephone with computer back-up."

"How did the managers like the training?"

"They loved it," said the entrepreneur.

"That's exciting," said the author. "So you essentially have a division of your company that's run by people with a positive, possibility filtering system for the future."

"Yes, we do," said the entrepreneur.

Once again the author pulled out his notebook. "We've talked about negative filtering as the second reason people don't put their know-how into action," he said as he glanced at his notes. "I think I get how listening with a positive mind-set and using Green Light Thinking help people overcome that. I'm ready to learn about the third and final reason."

REASON 3:
Lack of Follow-Up

"**Y**ou're still an eager learner!" said the entrepreneur with a laugh. "Sounds like you're really getting some value out of what you've been learning."

"I am," said the author, "even beyond my golf game. The idea of actually applying and benefiting from everything I learn is very appealing. According to my notes here, you said the third reason people don't put their knowledge into action is lack of follow-up."

"Yes," said Phil. "Since some people, after they are exposed to something new, don't have a follow-up plan, guess what happens?"

"I bet they revert back to old habits," said the author.

"Bingo," said Phil. "People need a follow-up plan to put their know-how into action. That's exactly what I did with Suzanne. After I convinced her that she had a negative filtering system that made her a wet blanket for new ideas, if I hadn't put a follow-up plan together, I doubt if any change would have occurred. She might have tried to listen more openly for a while, but eventually her old habit would have taken over."

The author nodded. "That reminds me of something Peter Drucker was quoted as saying: 'Nothing good happens by accident.'"

"That's so true," said Phil. "To change behavior and get the results you want you need structure, support, and accountability. When all three of those are in place, you have a good follow-up plan. The third reason people don't put their know-how into action—lack of follow-up—is the most difficult roadblock of all. That's why you need a plan."

"Why do you say it's the most difficult roadblock?" asked the author.

"Let me start with some historical background," Phil replied with a thoughtful look. "I learned the importance of having a good follow-up strategy from my father. He was a master cabinetmaker from Germany. He told me again and again never to take a job unless I was willing to be mentored."

"What did he mean by that?" the author asked.

"He meant that he wanted me to be willing to work under somebody who really knew how to do what I wanted to learn. My father was the best teacher I've ever had or ever known. His follow-up learning system was simple. He would:

Tell me

Show me

Let me

Correct me

Tell me

Show me

Let me

Correct me

Tell me...

"He would do this over and over again—our old friend repetition—until he hammered home whatever he was telling or showing me," continued Phil. "For example, my first bike. We picked it up at the junkyard, hauled it home, and took it apart. He showed me how to put it back together again—how to fix the brakes, build a gear, put new spokes on the wheels, and give it a complete overhaul. Then, to my dismay, after we had it all put back together, he made me take it all apart again. I did it over and over to the point that I could almost put it together with my eyes closed."

"That must have been some experience," said the author. "He certainly provided structure and accountability."

"He certainly did," said Phil. "My dad was instinctively doing the right thing. He was following up on what he'd showed me. His system made sure that I understood the correct way of doing something from the very start."

"I get that," said the author. "Without immediate follow up after being exposed to new ways of doing something, you will revert back to your old habits."

"What really helps," said Phil, "is to start practicing right away. The quicker you use a newly acquired skill, the more likely it is that you'll master it.

"But remember," said the entrepreneur, "make sure that when you're practicing, you're doing it the right way. As my father put it:

Practice Doesn't
Make Perfect.
Perfect Practice
Makes Perfect.

"All this talk of practicing a new skill right away reminds me of school," said the author. "I don't know how many times I wound up cramming for an exam. If I had simply gone over my notes on a day-to-day basis, cramming for an exam would have been unnecessary. When I crammed, I was essentially learning the content all over again. I always did better if I kept up with the work."

"It was the same with repairing bicycles," said Phil. "My father's follow-up plan was to get me practicing the skills as soon as possible, as much as possible, and then hold me accountable for my performance. He supervised my practicing until he felt I could do it on my own."

"Even during your rebellious teens?" asked the author.

"Even then," replied the entrepreneur. "When I was a teen, my dad bought me an old car that we had to have towed home. I didn't know the difference between the transmission and the master cylinder or the headers and the exhaust pipes. I was a complete novice. Together we took each section apart, and then he'd tell me, show me, let me, correct me, et cetera, until I knew how to put each piece back together. And then guess what? He would take it completely apart again and say with a smile, 'Put it together and it's yours.'"

"I bet that was a challenge," said the author.

"It sure was," said the entrepreneur. "But can you imagine how psyched I was to do it right? My dad really turned me on to the fact that learning doesn't just happen in your head, it happens when you have a plan to help you do something with what you know. I've become a lifelong learner because I now believe:

Successful
People
Yearn to Learn
And
Have a Plan
For Learning

"Unless people are motivated to learn to do something and have a plan to do it right, it isn't very likely they'll hang in there and learn how to do it well. My dad created a need and a plan for me to merge with that car. It was part of me. One of my saddest memories is the day I joined the military and sold my ancient Model A."

"How about after you left home?" asked the author. "Were you able to stick with the follow-up habit you learned from your father?"

"I was," said Phil with a smile. "When I arrived at Fort Jackson, South Carolina, I set records taking machinery apart and putting it back together, starting with a rifle. I could do it faster and better than anyone, thanks to my dad. In many ways it's the secret to all of my success and to the creation of our training and development programs. If you can't use what you know, what good is it?"

"I hear the pride in your voice and the gratitude to your father," said the author, "but I didn't hear you mention much about support. Isn't that the third ingredient for an effective follow-up plan?"

Phil Murray's face became very somber. "Guilty as charged. While my father wanted me to succeed, gave me plenty of structure, and held me accountable for my performance, I wouldn't describe him as a supportive person."

"So he never caught you doing something right?" asked the author.

"Why do you put it that way?" asked Phil.

"Of all the things I've ever taught or written about, the most important to me is the power of catching people doing things right," said the author. "To me, the key to helping people develop and creating a great organization is to accentuate the positive. When it comes to training people and helping them develop, I always tell managers, 'Don't wait until people do things exactly right before you praise them.' In the beginning, their performance may be only approximately right. But that should be praised. Praise progress, because you're dealing with a moving target. Then you can correct them or, as I would say, redirect them so they can continue to improve."

"I hear what you're saying, but that wasn't my father's way," said Phil. "While I know my father wanted me to be successful, he never, using your terms, caught me doing something right. He always jumped to how I could do it better. It was years before I realized the negative impact that had on me."

"How so?" asked the author.

"It affected my relationships, for one thing," the entrepreneur said slowly. "When I was selling insurance, I recruited several hundred agents in one year. As you can imagine, I had a lot of training to do, telling, showing, letting, and correcting. One day an agent leaned over and said, 'Phil, an occasional pat on the back would be good for everyone.'"

"How did you respond?" asked the author.

"I thought long and hard about it," said Phil. "I realized right away that he was right, but I needed to figure out how to do it."

"Don't feel like the only one," said the author. "Most of us are much better at catching each other doing things wrong rather than right."

"I realize that now," said the entrepreneur, "but I also learned that if people are deprived of praising, either they give up trying and never are very successful, or they become driven."

"Driven? Really?"

"Yes," said the entrepreneur, "I am almost possessed by the desire to achieve and be successful. What I finally realized is that I am still looking for my father's approval."

"That highlights my problem with your father's follow-up plan," said the author. "It has no step where the person gets an 'atta boy' or an 'atta girl.' After the 'Let me' step I would have expected a 'Praise my progress' step before the 'Correct me' step."

"You're right. My father's follow-up system should have included a positive step, but that was not his way. We actually do have that important step when we use the follow-up system with our people. And that's the result of our brave HR director, Herb Goodson, who confronted me on it and insisted it be changed. Thanks to Herb, we now use all three techniques to help people get past the problem of lack of follow-up. Besides providing necessary structure and accountability, our company follow-up plan includes support by accentuating the positive."

"I'd love to talk to Herb," said the author.

"Great idea," said the entrepreneur. "You know how to make that happen. I'll talk to you later."

ACCENTUATING THE POSITIVE
TO HELP PEOPLE WIN

Later that morning the author knocked on the door of Herb's office. Herb obviously knew in advance that the author was coming, because he looked up and said, "I understand you like to catch people doing things right."

"I certainly do," replied the author. "I love the entrepreneur's idea that to really learn how to do something, you have to be willing to be coached and study under a master. But I feel the follow-up system he got from his father—tell me, show me, let me, correct me, et cetera—doesn't accentuate the positive. He told me you confronted him on the lack of support and the learning system you use in the company now includes catching people doing things right. I'd be interested in learning about that."

"Be happy to share what we're doing," said Herb. "First, let me give you a little background. We hire two kinds of people: winners and potential winners. Winners are people who are already experienced in what we have hired them to do and have a good performance track record."

"They don't need much help, do they?" guessed the author.

"You're absolutely right," insisted Herb. "In their competency area they are already up to speed. They merely need to understand our business and culture a little more if they are new to the organization, and they need to be clear on their goals."

"Plus, know what good behavior looks like," added the author.

"Right," said Herb. "They need to know when they've hit a home run. Once they know about our business and are clear on our goals and standards, they don't have to be coached much anymore. Rather than master teachers, they need master cheerleaders."

"Tell me about what you do with the potential winners you hire," said the author.

"These are people we think can become winners if we properly train them," said Herb.

"So you don't hire any losers, do you?" said the author with a smile.

"No, we try to avoid that," said Herb with a laugh. "We want everyone to have a chance to win. With our potential winners, the big thing we want to check is whether they have a positive attitude toward learning."

"I bet that means you check your winners for any stinkin' thinkin', doesn't it?" asked the author.

"It sure does," said Herb. "Phil insists that we give everyone we hire a check-up from the neck up and get rid of any stinkin' thinkin'. Once we know we have the right people on the bus, we zero in on our potential winners. First, we design a personalized training for them that includes some of our own offerings as well as training we contract from the outside. We want to jump-start their learning."

"Is that where you begin to implement your follow-up system?"

"Yes," said Herb. "With all the training we do, we want our people to go well beyond mere theory and knowledge. They must have opportunities to practice using what they are taught. When I got the go-ahead from Phil, we changed our follow-up learning system to:

tell me

show me

let me

observe me

praise my progress and / or redirect me

tell me

show me

let me

observe me

praise my progress and / or redirect me

78

"You'll notice we added one new step—'observe me'—in addition to changing 'correct me' to 'praise me and/or redirect me,'" continued Herb.

"That's so consistent with my thinking," said the author. "But to praise or redirect people, the manager has to be around."

"You're right. To praise or redirect people, managers have to be around to observe people's progress," said Herb. "In the old days when people were learning, they worked alongside a master. Everything they did was observed by the master. Today in the world of work, things are moving so fast that managers often are not around when their people are first trying to use their new knowledge."

"And that leads to managerial seagull behavior," said the author with a smile. "When the learner makes a mistake—particularly if it reflects on the manager in the department—the manager flies in, makes a lot of noise, dumps on the learner, and then flies out."

"I never quite heard it expressed that way," said Herb with a laugh, "but that's what we want to avoid. We want our master teachers—whether they are managers or not—to work closely with potential winners, particularly when they are first trying to do what they have been taught."

"Does a person's manager always have to be a master teacher when that person is learning a new skill?"

"Not always," said Herb, "but it is the responsibility of a manager to make sure every one of their people has a teacher or coach if they need it."

"People management certainly takes a lot of time and effort, doesn't it?" said the author.

"It does, and it should," said Herb. "But let me explain a few things. The most critical periods are when people have just been to training or are attempting to do something new. Too often when people are sent to training, when they get back, nobody knows or cares that they have been gone. As a result, their workload piles up during their absence, and there is little time to focus on applying what they have been taught, particularly in a non-technical area like leadership or team building, or a skill area like listening and praising. Since we don't send people to a lot of training in our company and want them to learn less more, we want to get a bang for our buck."

"So you really focus on managing and coaching after training," said the author.

"Yes. One other thing that's important to know is that you don't *tell me, show me, let me, observe me, praise my progress and/or redirect me* forever. Over time, your teaching style should noticeably move to *ask me, let me show you so you can observe me, and then praise me.*"

"And eventually," said the author, "it should move to *tell myself, perform, and praise or redirect my own progress.*"

"Absolutely," said Herb. "Eventually you want learners to become masters in what they do so they can handle a delegating leadership style, where their manager lets them run with the ball. Then they can manage themselves as well as coach others."

"I can see you don't leave closing the knowing-doing gap to chance," said the author. "When I talked to Phil, he said there were three key ingredients to an effective follow-up plan: structure, support, and accountability. It seems to me that all three are involved in your follow-up learning system."

"Absolutely," said Herb. "Through Phil's influence, we've learned that being an effective teacher or manager is more of a discipline than an art. When it comes to helping people put their know-how into action, this is where all three ingredients have to be present."

"So that's all it takes to close the knowing-doing gap—a simple follow-up plan?" asked the author.

PROVIDING MORE STRUCTURE, SUPPORT, AND ACCOUNTABILITY

"Yes and no," said Herb. "I'm sure Phil told you that the third reason people don't do what they know—lack of follow-up—is the toughest hurdle to overcome. So we have several follow-up systems to make sure that people act on what they know."

The author got out his notebook, sensing that this might be some of the most valuable information he'd heard yet.

"I'll give you two examples," Herb continued. "First, we have implemented a one-on-one process in our organization. We require every manager to meet once every two weeks with each of his or her direct reports for fifteen to thirty minutes."

"Who sets the agenda?" asked the author.

"The direct report," said Herb. "It usually focuses on how they are doing on their goals and what, if any, help they need. But direct reports can discuss anything they want. It's their meeting."

"That's real support," said the author.

"It also provides structure and accountability," said Herb. "Since managers meet twenty-six times a year with each of their direct reports, that provides plenty of structure. Because of these frequent meetings, when it comes to an annual performance review, there are no surprises. Accountability is built in to the one-on-one process, and that has a tremendous impact on our company's performance and the retention of good people."

"How did you get managers to do one-on-ones?" asked the author. "That's quite a commitment of time and energy."

"Repetition, repetition, repetition," replied Herb. "Phil is almost like a third grade teacher. He says over and over again how important our one-on-one meetings are. It's like water torture. He also rewards those managers and direct reports who are holding these meetings."

"Both?"

"Absolutely," said Herb. "We don't permit our people to place the blame for things not happening up the hierarchy. Managing people is a partnership. So about 20 percent of everyone's performance evaluation is focused on their one-on-one meetings."

"That's a departure from the customary top-down management style," said the author.

"Yes, but we think it's necessary in order to close the knowing-doing gap and have a high-performing organization."

"You said you had a second example of the kind of structure and accountability you provide," said the author.

"We do," said Herb. "We believe in the power of outside coaches. For a minimum of six weeks after a major training program, we assign every participant a telephone coach. These are people, certified as coaches, who do not work at our company. As a result, they are not emotionally involved in the day-to-day pressures facing our people. All they are interested in is helping close our post-seminar knowing-doing gap."

"I would imagine that's extremely helpful," said the author.

"It is," said Herb. "We've found that after one of our leadership training programs, if participants have telephone coaching sessions for fifty minutes once a week for six weeks with an outside coach, they get the structure, support, and accountability they need, and we get the results we want. Adding one-on-one meetings to the mix is a powerful one-two follow-up punch to help people use what they've been taught. When people use what they've been taught and hit their goals and targets, everyone wins."

The author thanked Herb for his time. As he headed back to the entrepreneur's office for one last visit, his thoughts turned to his golf game. To improve, he knew that even if he went to Denny's golf school, he would need some kind of follow-up plan. Maybe that's something he could teach Mr. Know-It-All, so his friend didn't slowly start to revert to old habits. No matter how great the school was, a follow-up plan was essential.

Realizing the power of what he'd just been told by Herb, the author stopped to jot down some notes in clear, readable handwriting:

Reason Why People Don't Put
Their Know-How into Action #3:
Lack of Follow-Up

◆ Successful people yearn to learn and have a follow-up plan for learning.

◆ Doing what we've been taught cannot be left to chance. A follow-up plan that provides structure, support and accountability must be set up to help us behave on our good intentions.

◆ The sequence of *tell me, show me, let me, observe me, and praise my progress or redirect me* is a simple but powerful follow-up plan that helps potential winners become winners.

◆ Accentuating the positive helps learners become eager beavers. Praising progress is important before redirecting or correcting takes place. Over time, learners should be able to praise and redirect themselves.

◆ One-on-one meetings and outside telephone coaching are also helpful vehicles for closing the knowing-doing gap.

When the author approached the entrepreneur's office, Phil Murray was out front talking to Evelyn. He looked up and smiled.

"I'll bet you feel a lot better now that you know our follow-up system is more positive."

"I do," said the author as they entered Phil's office together.

"Are the principles of providing structure, support, and accountability the most important aspects of closing the knowing-doing gap?" the author asked.

"In many ways, they are," replied the entrepreneur. "But remember that our follow-up system builds on the first two reasons that we discussed, information overload and negative filtering. Until you decide to focus on a few things to learn and get rid of your stinkin' thinkin', our positive follow-up system will not have as much impact. Yet it is the bridge that connects the knowing-doing gap and makes our programs successful."

"I get it now," said the author. "Few people will ever change by reading a book, listening to an audio, watching a video, or attending a one-time seminar. You have to roll up your sleeves and become a focused learner. Then you have to filter the new information through a positive mind-set, and, finally, you have to have a plan for putting your new knowledge into practice right away."

"That's a good summary," said Phil. "Let me share one last thing. There is a golden thread that runs through the life of every high achiever. It is the golden thread of focus, backed by persistence. In one way or another, every person of extraordinary accomplishment has the ability to focus on a target with laserlike intensity, staying on course to achieve the goal."

"That's what I'm worried about—my own ability to focus and follow up," said the author. "I'm concerned that I won't be able to stick with what you've taught me. I feel like I need a master teacher who can coach me and give me the structure, support, and accountability I need."

Phil smiled brightly. "I never thought you'd ask. Why don't we check with each other once every two weeks for fifteen to thirty minutes on the telephone so you can share with me how you're doing and what additional help you need?"

"So you're willing to do telephone one-on-ones with me?"

"Yes, I am," said Phil, "if you promise me one thing."

"What's that?" asked the author.

"Promise me that once you've been able to implement all the things we've talked about—you are focused on a few things to learn, you have an open mind, and you have a clear follow-up plan. You will:

Share What
You've Learned
And
Teach Others.

EPILOGUE

Phil and the author kept in contact through their biweekly telephone calls. The author shared with him everything that was happening in his life, including reports about his time at the golf school his friend, Denny, had recommended. They spent two calls designing his follow-up plan, so that he would not revert back to his old golfing habits. These discussions reminded them both that closing the knowing-doing gap has no boundaries. It can impact every part of one's life.

During one of their calls, the author invited Phil to sit in on a convention speech he was giving in town. Phil jumped at the opportunity, particularly when the author told him the title of his speech was "Putting Your Know-How into Action."

"What a great topic," Phil said to the author. "Did you ever think of calling your speech 'Know Can Do'?"

"Not until you mentioned it," said the author with a laugh. "But I realize that teaching others what I know is one of the best ways to begin to apply new knowledge, and that process deepens my commitment to putting my know-how into action."

"That's right," Phil replied. "Closing the knowing-doing gap is more action than words."

Several weeks later, when Phil arrived at the convention center, the organizers had a nametag for him at the registration desk. He found out that this was an annual gathering of ASTD, an international organization of people in the training and development field. *A perfect audience for closing the knowing-doing gap*, thought the entrepreneur.

When Phil entered the convention hall, it was already jammed with people. The author's speech was the opening keynote for the convention. Phil guessed there were several thousand people in attendance. He wandered down the aisle and smiled when he found a seat near the front. He firmly believed that people who sat in the front of the class always learned more.

After some opening music and fanfare, the president of ASTD entered the stage from the rear and made his way to the podium. He welcomed everyone and talked about some major highlights of the convention. Then he turned his attention to introducing the author. Even Phil was impressed with the author's credentials. He learned some new things about his friend.

After a polite, welcoming applause, the author moved to center stage. He smiled as he thanked the president for his kind introduction. "My father would have enjoyed it, and my mother would have believed it," he quipped.

Getting serious, the author opened his remarks. "We have a crisis in our training and development field. What we teach is seldom practiced or used. People today know a lot more about leadership and management than anyone ever sees. The gap between knowing and doing is probably wider than the gap between ignorance and knowledge. This bothered me for a long time, until I recently learned about the missing link—repetition, repetition, repetition. That's what I want to share with you this morning.

"In our field, for years we have defined learning as a change in behavior. Yet we have not agreed on how to make that happen. We all know change is not easy, particularly changing one's own behavior.

"There are actually three levels of change when you move from knowing something to doing something. The first level of change is at the knowledge level. It's the easiest and least time consuming thing to change in people. All you have to do is read a new book, listen to a new audio, watch a new video, or go to a new seminar. So it's very attractive.

"That leads to the first reason people don't do what they know. It's more fun to learn something new than to struggle to do what you know. As a result, we have information overload. We're drowning in a sea of information. But unlike a fish, we don't have a built-in monitoring system that can take from the water what we need and leave what we don't. What's the answer here? It's repetition, repetition, repetition. We have to focus our energy on a few things, rather than a lot of things.

"How many diets does it take to lose weight? Only the one you stick to. We have to stop always looking for the next new management concept and follow up on the one we just taught people. I'll never forget being asked to speak to all of the managers in a company. The president wouldn't let me on the stage, though, until I had come to their corporate headquarters and found out what they had already been teaching these leaders. He told me, 'I want you to build on what we have been teaching, not send us off in a new direction.'

"In reflecting on my experience with that president, I realized how important top management support is in closing the knowing-doing gap. He was a stickler for focusing people's energy. He even went as far as asking every person in the company to identify one thing they would be able to add to their résumé the next year that hadn't been there the previous year. He thought everyone should learn something new every year, not a lot of things every year.

"So the key to overcoming the first reason why people don't do what they know—information over-load—is to apply the less-more philosophy. Focus on less, and repeat it again and again. Focus, focus."

The words were just flowing out of the author. His command of the subject surprised even him. *I hope I can help them put this good stuff into action*, he thought.

Then he had an idea.

"Before I tell you about the second level of change," the author continued, "let me ask you to do a couple of things. Stand up, all of you."

As the crowd got to their feet, the author said, "I'm going to ask you to do two things. First what I'd like you to do is wander around this hall for about thirty seconds and greet as many people as you possibly can. But greet them in a special way. Greet them as if they are insignificant and you are looking for someone much more important to talk to."

After everyone laughed, they began to wander around the hall, ignoring each other. After a while, the author shouted out, "Stop where you are, but don't sit down."

When the crowd had quieted down, the author said, "Now wander around for another thirty seconds, but this time, greet people as if they are a long-lost friend and you are glad to see them."

With that, a tremendous burst of energy filled the hall as people laughed, smiled, and hugged each other. After a while, the author shouted, "You can all sit down now."

When the crowd was finally settled, he smiled and said, "Why do you think I asked you to do that, besides the fact that I'm from California? Pretty soon we'll be bringing in some hot tubs."

Everyone laughed.

"Seriously," said the author, "the reason I had you do those two exercises was to show that to be a great leader and successful person, you need to know how to manage people's energy, including your own. Of the two activities I put you through, which one created more energy in the room?"

Everyone shouted out, "The second activity!"

With that the author said, "What did I do to change the energy in the room? All I did was change what you were thinking about from a negative thought—these are unimportant people—to a positive thought—these are long-lost friends whom I'm really glad to see. With that, the whole energy in the room changed.

"How many of you know that the computer and the brain have a lot in common?" asked the author. A few tentative hands went up. "Both the computer and the brain don't know the difference between the truth and what you tell them. When you put information in a computer, it doesn't say, 'Where'd you get those facts? Those facts are wrong.' The computer does whatever it can with the information you give it. For years we've said about the computer, 'Garbage in'—"

The crowd yelled out, "Garbage out!"

"Absolutely," said the author. "The brain is the same way. It doesn't know the difference between the truth and what you tell it. Suppose you got up this morning, looked in the mirror, and said, 'You're fabulous.' Your brain wouldn't say, 'You've got to be kidding. I know you better than that.'"

The crowd roared.

"You see," said the author, "successful people know how to program their minds in positive ways.

"This leads me to the second level of change that we have to go through if we are to behave differently. It's called *attitudinal change*. An attitude is an emotionally charged bit of knowledge. It's when you feel strongly in a positive or negative way towards something that you know. Attitudes are tougher to change than knowledge, because you can say, 'I know what you're saying, *but*....' That's why we have to get rid of people's stinkin' thinkin' by dealing with their negative filtering system—the second reason people don't do what they know. We do this by helping them develop a positive filtering system. Without an open attitude toward learning, you're never going to close the knowing-doing gap."

The author paused to take a drink from the water glass on the podium.

"Most of us," he continued, "when we sit in an audience like today, are skeptical. Why? Because as we were growing up, our parents and other adults tended to accent the negative, rather than the positive. When we had an idea we were excited about, they usually threw a wet blanket on it. As a result, we started to adopt that way of thinking, too. What we all need to become are Green Light thinkers. When we hear something, our first response should be, 'How can I use this? What will I gain if I learn it?' We have to stay positive as we are learning. If we don't, our 'yes, but' attitude will kill everything that comes our way.

"Let me see if I can summarize what I've said to this point. Since changing our knowledge is the easiest change to make, it is a temptation to start taking on a lot more new information, which leads to information overload. Then attitude change comes into play. Since it's more difficult than changing knowledge, it's more involved. Changing our negative filtering system is not easy. The third and most difficult level of change is behavior change, the very meaning of learning. Why is this so difficult? Because now you have to do something.

"For example, for years I knew that I was twenty-five to thirty pounds overweight. I was always trying this diet and that diet, without any luck. What I finally realized is that if I was going to make a difference in my health, particularly around my weight, I had to focus on it. I really needed help.

"It's difficult to change something when you've been doing it for a long time. I grew up in a Jewish community. I used to fantasize at night that I would be locked in a Jewish delicatessen. I can smell a piece of cheesecake a mile away! With that mindset, you can imagine how hard it was to change my behavior around eating.

"Changing your behavior is tough, even when you know you should and you have a positive attitude about it, which I always had around my eating.

You need a real concentrated follow-up effort. Most people have not developed such a strategy. That's the third reason people don't do what they know—they lack a follow-up system. To get the results you want—put your know-how into action—you need a follow-up plan that provides structure, support, and accountability.

"Structure means regularly scheduled meetings with a coach, a support group, or some vehicle that will help you behave on your good intentions. Unless you have that, you know where the road paved by good intentions will lead.

"Helpful structure is driven by relationships. When the people who meet with you care about you, they will give you the support you need and, in a loving way, hold you accountable.

"When I finally had all that in place, I was able to conquer my weight problem. Now I have a nutrition coach, an exercise coach, and a life coach—people who work with me on an ongoing basis—supporting me and monitoring what I do. All my coaches realize that the reason New Year's resolutions don't work is that if we could accomplish them without help, they wouldn't be resolutions. Inevitably, when we announce a New Year's resolution, all the important people in our lives laugh and say, 'I'll believe it when I see it.' They go to a leave-alone, delegating leadership style, waiting for us to fail. And of course, we always do.

"What we need to do in the training business is to spend ten times the amount of time following up our training as we do organizing, developing, and delivering it. What we need are mentors and coaches to help people move from being novices in doing what they know to becoming master teachers."

The author went on eloquently, giving all kinds of examples of how focus, repetition, positive thinking, and a follow-up structure changed people's lives. As he ended his speech, he could feel the positive energy coming from the audience. He had really hit a home run.

"I can see that some of you are really excited about what I have been sharing with you this morning. So am I. In fact, if none of you have gotten anything out of this session, I needed it. It gave me a chance to remind myself what I have to do to close my own knowing-doing gaps."

With that, the author had everybody in the audience stand up. With a smile, he said, "Take your right hand and put it on your left shoulder and take your left hand and put it on your right shoulder, and give yourself a hug. You're fabulous, and I know you're now going to be able to put your know-how into action."

With everyone standing and hugging themselves, the author quipped, "What a great way to get a standing ovation." Laughter filled the auditorium. As the author looked over the audience, he spotted the entrepreneur sitting near the front.

As everyone was taking their seats, he said, "I would be remiss to end my talk without introducing to you the person who broke the code for me." The author gestured for Phil to stand and be acknowledged. "Please, everyone, let's give a big round of applause to Phil Murray, entrepreneur extraordinaire."

Reluctantly, Phil got to his feet. He had a big grin on his face as he waved to the crowd.

My friend really got it, Phil thought with pride and joy. *He's not only teaching others how to do what they know, he's putting it to work in his own life.*

ACKNOWLEDGMENTS

W̲e give our wholehearted praise and acknowledgment to

Margie Blanchard and Garry Demarest, who taught us about one-on-ones;

Margie Blanchard, Eunice Parisi-Carew, Lily Guthrie, Francisco Gomez, and Jason Arnold for teaching us about the power of the Office of the Future;

Scott Blanchard and Madeleine Homan for what they taught us about the importance of follow-up coaching;

Edward deBono for his six hats philosophy of conceptual thinking and his idea that it's better to focus on one kind of thinking at a time;

Paul Hersey for his early recognition of Ken's writing ability and for teaching us about the levels of change;

Wendy Wong for coming up with a great title;

Raz Ingracsci and The Hoffman Process for teaching us the impact our early childhood experience with adults has on our thinking;

Charlie Tremendous Jones for exciting us about the importance of reading;

Walter Pauk, author of *How to Study in College*, for what he taught us about the importance of note taking in becoming true learners;

Norman Vincent Peale for what he taught us about the power of positive thinking;

Jeffrey Pfeffer and Robert Sutton for their pioneering classic, *The Knowing-Doing Gap*;

John Darling, Kathy Daugherty, Dave Emerick, Dean Lind, Lynn Marriott, Kip Puterbaugh, Tom Wischmeyer, and Dave Witt, the golf pros at the Golf University, for all they taught us about learning the great game of golf;

Don Shula for teaching us the importance of repetition, so people know their job so well they can go on automatic pilot and make something big happen;

Rick Tate and Gary Heil for their original work on legendary service, Sheldon Bowles for his thinking about creating Raving Fans, and Kathy Cuff and Cathy Huett for taking these concepts to a new level;

Zig Ziglar for helping us understand the importance of giving people a check-up from the neck up and getting rid of any stinkin' thinkin';

Bob Davis, former general manager of Chevron, for reminding us that praising progress is important, because it's a moving target;

Jim Collins, for helping us understand what makes great leaders;

Ken Blanchard's wife, Margie, for always being there for him, and his family—Scott Blanchard, Madeleine Homan, Debbie Blanchard, Humberto Medina, and Tom McKee—for their leadership of The Ken Blanchard Companies, which has permitted Ken to focus on projects like this wonderful book;

Paul Meyer's wife, Jane, for letting him stay focused yet making sure he still had a balanced life; his father, August Carl Meyer, a German cabinetmaker who was the greatest teacher Paul has known in his lifetime—much of what is continued in this book was a result of his father's masterful teaching;

Dick Ruhe's wife, Cathy Ruhe, and their sons Richard, Michael, and Christopher for their whole-hearted support through the years; to Dick's father Richard E. Ruhe Sr. for teaching him about dealing with life; and to his class advisor, Leslie High, who was his first role model of leadership and influence in organizations.

ABOUT THE AUTHORS

Ken Blanchard

Few people have created a more positive impact on the day-to-day management of people than Ken Blanchard, a prominent, gregarious, sought-after author, speaker, and consultant. Ken is universally characterized by friends, colleagues, and clients as one of the most insightful, powerful, and compassionate men in business today.

Famous for making the seemingly complex simple, Ken coauthored *The One Minute Manager*® with Spencer Johnson. That book has sold more than thirteen million copies, is still on best-seller lists, and has been translated into more than twenty-five languages. He is the author of more than forty books with total sales of more than eighteen million copies. His recent best sellers include *Raving Fans!*® and *Gung Ho!*®, coauthored with Sheldon Bowles and *Whale Done!*, coauthored with Chuck Tompkins, Thad Lacinak, and Jim Ballard.

Ken serves as the Chief Spiritual Officer of The Ken Blanchard Companies, Inc., an international management training and consulting firm that he and his wife, Dr. Marjorie Blanchard, founded in 1979 in San Diego, California. He is also cofounder of the Lead Like Jesus Ministries, a nonprofit organization committed to helping people become servant leaders.

Paul J. Meyer

A celebrated trailblazer and leader of the multi-billion-dollar self-improvement industry, Paul J. Meyer founded Success Motivation Institute, Inc., in 1960 and dedicated it to "motivating people to their full potential." Based on Meyer's vision to help people achieve their goals, his flagship company has grown into an international group of companies marketing his materials in more than sixty countries and in twenty-three languages with others in progress. Combined sales exceed $2 billion worldwide, which surpasses the sales of any other self-improvement author, living or deceased.

Success in his own life and expertise in teaching others to fulfill their potential and reach their goals has earned Meyer worldwide recognition and a position of international prominence. With a rich background of experience and success, Meyer reveals many of his success principles in his book *Fortune, Family & Faith*. Other books authored by Meyer include the *New York Times* best seller *Chicken Soup for the Golden Soul*, *The 5 Pillars of Leadership*, *I Inherited a Fortune!*, *Unlocking Your Legacy*, *Forgiveness . . . The Ultimate Miracle*, *24 Keys That Bring Complete Success*, and *Become the Coach You Were Meant to Be*. A book written about Meyer, *Paul J. Meyer and the Art of Giving*, illustrates Meyer's principles for stewardship and giving.

Dick Ruhe

Dick Ruhe is a highly popular motivational speaker, a celebrated consultant and a gifted trainer. His highly spirited presentations connect with audiences at a core level, and his humor often brings down the house.

As a senior consulting partner for The Ken Blanchard Companies, Dick is the author of the training program *Total Quality Leadership*. He has also worked with Tom Peters, Gordon Lippit, and Paul Hersey. He has served as a regular columnist for *Sales and Marketing* magazine and has been published in *Training and Development*, *Proceedings of the Academy of Management*, and *Executive Excellence*.

111

Dick received his MBA from the University of New Haven and his doctorate in human resource development from George Washington University. He is the author of *Getting Major Results*, a field book for change and leadership.

SERVICES AVAILABLE

For more than 27 years, The Ken Blanchard Companies® has been in the business of helping people put their knowledge into action. The mission of the company is to unleash the potential and power of people and organizations for the greater good. Based on the belief that people are the key to accomplising strategic objectives and driving business results, Blanchard® programs develop excellence in leadership, teams, customer loyalty, change management, and performance improvement. The company's world-class trainers and coaches drive organizational and behavioral change at all levels and help people make the shift from knowing to doing.

The company has delivered training and performance improvement best practices in more than 50 countries. Blanchard consulting partners are available for training initiatives, consulting engagements, and keynote addresses around the world.

Global Headquarters
The Ken Blanchard Companies
125 State Place
Escondido, CA 92029
www.kenblanchard.com
(800) 728-6000 from the United States
(760) 489-5005 from anywhere

The **Meyer family companies** were built using the power of spaced repetition. Combined sales have exceeded $2 billion, a testament to the efficacy of the concept.

Leadership Management,® Inc.—
For more than forty years, LMI has been one of the premier leadership and management companies in the United States.
www.lmi-usa.com

Leadership Management® International, Inc.—
Similar to our U.S. company, although Leadership Management International operates only outside the United States. Programs are marketed in twenty-four languages and in sixty countries.
www.lmi-inc.com

Success Motivation® International, Inc.—
This personal development company produces
goal setting, motivation, and attitude programs.
www.success-motivation.com

Creative Education Institute®—
A company that has helped more than three million
public and private school children who have
learning disabilities.
www.ceilearning.com

Paul J. Meyer Resources is the exclusive source
for Paul J. Meyer books, booklets, CDs and DVDs.
www.paulj.meyer.com

About Berrett-Koehler Publishers

Berrett-Koehler is an independent publisher dedicated to an ambitious mission: Creating a World that Works for All.

We believe that to truly create a better world, action is needed at all levels — individual, organizational, and societal. At the individual level, our publications help people align their lives with their values and with their aspirations for a better world. At the organizational level, our publications promote progressive leadership and management practices, socially responsible approaches to business, and humane and effective organizations. At the societal level, our publications advance social and economic justice, shared prosperity, sustainability, and new solutions to national and global issues.

A major theme of our publications is "Opening Up New Space." They challenge conventional thinking, introduce new ideas, and foster positive change. Their common quest is changing the underlying beliefs, mindsets, institutions, and structures that keep generating the same cycles of problems, no matter who our leaders are or what improvement programs we adopt.

We strive to practice what we preach—to operate our publishing company in line with the ideas in our books. At the core of our approach is *stewardship*, which we define as a deep sense of responsibility to administer the company for the benefit of all of our "stakeholder" groups: authors, customers, employees, investors, service providers, and the communities and environment around us.

We are grateful to the thousands of readers, authors, and other friends of the company who consider themselves to be part of the "BK Community." We hope that you, too, will join us in our mission.

Be Connected

Visit Our Website
Go to www.bkconnection.com to read exclusive previews and excerpts of new books, find detailed information on all Berrett-Koehler titles and authors, browse subject-area libraries of books, and get special discounts.

Subscribe to Our Free E-Newsletter
Be the first to hear about new publications, special discount offers, exclusive articles, news about bestsellers, and more! Get on the list for our free e-newsletter by going to www.bkconnection.com.

Get Quantity Discounts
Berrett-Koehler books are available at quantity discounts for orders of ten or more copies. Please call us toll-free at (800) 929-2929 or email us at bkp.orders@aidcvt.com.

Host a Reading Group
For tips on how to form and carry on a book reading group in your workplace or community, see our website at www.bkconnection.com.

Join the BK Community
Thousands of readers of our books have become part of the "BK Community" by participating in events featuring our authors, reviewing draft manuscripts of forthcoming books, spreading the word about their favorite books, and supporting our publishing program in other ways. If you would like to join the BK Community, please contact us at bkcommunity@bkpub.com.